President

Fiction and Nonfiction Paired Reading

If I Ran for
PRESIDENT
Catherine Stier

President
Heather Kissock

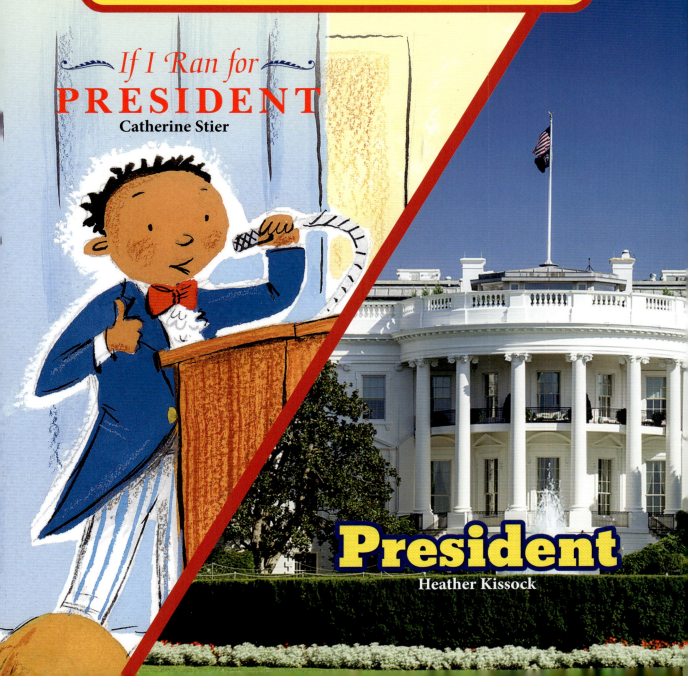

President
Fiction and Nonfiction Paired Reading

Go to www.openlightbox.com and enter this book's unique code.

BOOK CODE
AVJ47843

Explore your **AV2 Fiction** interactive eBook!

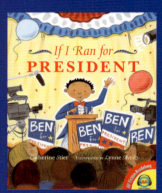

Imagine starring in commercials and traveling in your own campaign bus! Or seeing your face on bumper stickers and T-shirts! If you ran for president, you would get to do these and other fun things, but you would also have to do a lot of hard work. You would study the nation's problems, tell the American people about your platform, and much more.

If I Ran for President
First Published by
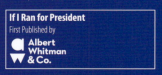

The Benefits of Paired Fiction and Nonfiction

Pairing fiction and nonfiction titles is a research-based educational approach proven to enhance student outcomes. It improves reading comprehension, increases engagement, expands background knowledge, and helps build vocabulary.

Each paired fiction title is read aloud by professional narrators, offering students the opportunity to listen and learn at their own pace. Every paired nonfiction title comes with a host of digital features designed to engage all learning styles and build a solid foundation for future growth. Both fiction and nonfiction titles are sure to captivate even the most reluctant reader with their dynamic visuals and curated content.

AV2 Fiction Readalong Navigation

1-Year Grades K–5 Premium Fiction Subscription ISBN
979-8-8745-1655-0

The digital components of this book are guaranteed to stay active for at least five years from the date of publication.

It's fun to imagine running for the highest office in the land—and maybe becoming president of the United States of America. After all, the president is famous, makes lots of important decisions, and lives in a really cool mansion.

There are rules written in our Constitution about who can be president. A person must be thirty-five years old, so a kid really couldn't be president. Also, a person running for president must be a citizen who was born in the United States and has lived here for at least fourteen years. That's it! You can be president if you are a man or a woman. You can be president whether your parents were born in the United States or anywhere else in the world.

When citizens vote in November every four years, they are not voting directly for president and vice-president even though they mark their candidates' names on the ballot. They are voting for a group of people from their state called *electors*. In December, the electors cast their states' official votes (called *electoral votes*) for president and vice-president. The formal announcement of the winners is not until January, but usually it's clear on election night in November who has won.

Each elector votes for the candidates who won the people's vote (called the *popular vote*) in his or her state. Each state has a set number of electors, equal to the number of its senators and representatives in Congress. Altogether, there are 538 electors (including 3 for Washington, D.C., although it is not a state). When a candidate has received 270 electoral votes, he or she has won the presidential or vice-presidential election. This complicated system, which we call the *electoral college*, is outlined in the Constitution.

Running for president is surely an exhausting but exciting time for a candidate. And who knows? Perhaps someday *you* will "toss your hat in the ring" to run for president of the United States of America!

It would be great to run for president of the United States!
If I ran for president, I'd hope the people of the United States would choose me for a very important job—the job of leading our country.

And I'd hope to follow in the footsteps of past presidents such as:
George Washington, our first president,
Thomas Jefferson,
Theodore Roosevelt,
and Abraham Lincoln.

I'd have to think carefully about my decision to run for president. I would want to know how my family felt about it, too.

Then I'd ask myself: "Am I the best person for the job? Am I ready to work VERY, VERY, VERY hard for my country? Do lots of people believe in me, and will they help me run for office?"

If I could answer yes to all those questions, then I'd declare my candidacy. That means I'd announce I was interested in the job of president of the United States.

If I ran for president, I'd run a campaign to let voters learn all about me. People who thought I would be a good president would donate money or time to help. I'd hire people to work on my campaign, too.

Campaigns can make a candidate famous! Soon my name or face would appear on signs,

buttons,

bumper stickers,

and T-shirts!

I'd even star in television commercials.

If I ran for president, I'd work with my political party—that's a group of people who share the same beliefs about how the country should be governed. They support candidates who uphold those ideas. The two major parties are the Democratic party (their symbol is a donkey) and the Republican party (their symbol is an elephant). There are other parties, too, called "third parties."

But people besides me would want to be president. The Republican and Democratic parties must choose whom they'll support in the election. In some states, like Iowa, the parties each hold meetings called caucuses (KAW-kuhs-uhs), where members pick their favorite candidate. In most states, party members hold an election called a primary.

Caucuses and primaries show which candidates are popular with voters and who might have the best chance of being elected president.
 The first primary is held in New Hampshire, in the winter before the presidential election. I'd be sure to visit there—but I'd have to bundle up!

In the summer before the election, the political parties announce their candidate for president. The major parties make this announcement at meetings called conventions. Each state sends delegates to the convention. Delegates vote for the candidate who was most popular in their state.

A convention looks like a big celebration, full of cheering and chanting, balloons and confetti. Millions of Americans watch the excitement on TV.

By the time of the convention, everyone usually knows which candidate will be chosen, but the delegates still hold a vote.

If my party chose me to run for president, I'd make a speech to get everyone excited about helping me win. I'd tell the American people about my platform—my plans and ideas for our country. My running mate would make a speech, too. That's the person who'd be my vice-president if I became president.

If I ran for president, I'd be invited to debate with other presidential candidates. A person called a moderator would ask us questions. People across the country would listen carefully to our answers.

Reporters would ask me questions, too, about my life, my family—even my kitten, Sassy.

They'd print old photographs of me in newspapers and magazines, like the snapshot of me in my superhero costume, or my baby picture when I still wore diapers!

If I ran for president, I would travel the country to meet lots of people. I'd have my own campaign bus or airplane to take me from place to place. Inside there'd be comfy seats, perfect for checking out the news, writing speeches, and thinking about how to solve the nation's problems.

I'd take naps, too—I'd need the extra rest!

I'd work hard and be very busy! All in one week,
I might share cereal with kindergartners in California,

crunch corn with farmers in Kansas,

... and have dinner in Delaware, where I'd order the Blue Plate Special with apple pie and a large strawberry milkshake. After all that food, I might not feel too well! Still, I'd have to smile and talk with the people I met.

Presidential candidates make lots of speeches, shake hands— and cuddle babies.

Finally, in November, Election Day would arrive. If I ran for president, I'd be nervous and excited!

On Election Day, millions of voters from across the country go to their polling places to "cast their ballots." That's another way to say that they vote.

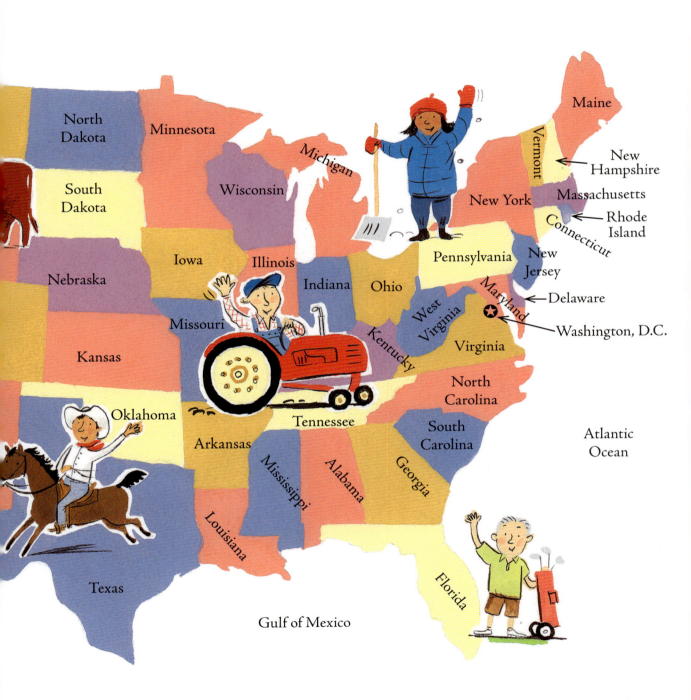

In our country, people vote in private. No one but you knows how you voted, but I know I'd choose my favorite candidate—me!

Once the voting is finished, officials count up the ballots. Then comes the announcement on television, radio, in the newspapers, and on the Internet. People everywhere find out who will be the next president of the United States. I'd stay up late and keep my fingers crossed.

If I ran for president and lost, the people who worked so hard on my campaign would be disappointed. I'd be disappointed, too! Still, I'd be proud that I had taken part in a free and fair election. I'd make a telephone call to offer my best wishes and my support to the winner—our next president!

But if I won ... WOW!

On January 20th, I'd say the words of the oath of office and be sworn in as president. On that day, my Inauguration Day, there'd be a parade and a fancy ball!

30

Then I'd move into the White House in Washington, D.C., to begin my four-year term as the president of the United States of America.

And what would I do when I became president? Well, that's another story.

President

Fiction and Nonfiction Paired Reading

Go to www.openlightbox.com and enter this book's unique code.

BOOK CODE
AVJ47843

Explore your **AV2 Nonfiction** interactive eBook!

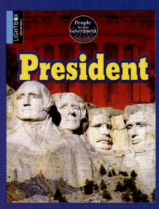

The president of the United States is the head of state. This means that he or she is the top leader in the country's government. Learn more in *President*, a title in the **People in Our Government** series.

President First Published by **LIGHTBOX**

AV2 Nonfiction Readalong Navigation

 AUDIO High-quality narration using text-to-speech system

VIDEOS Embedded high-definition video clips

 ACTIVITIES Printable PDFs that can be emailed and graded

 WEBLINKS Curated links to external, child-safe resources

SLIDESHOWS Pictorial overviews of key concepts

TRANSPARENCIES Step-by-step layering of maps, diagrams, charts, and timelines

INTERACTIVE MAPS Interactive maps and aerial satellite imagery

QUIZZES Ten multiple-choice questions that are automatically graded and emailed for teacher assessment

 KEY WORDS Matching key concepts to their definitions

1-Year Grades K–5 Premium Fiction Subscription ISBN
979-8-8745-1655-0

The digital components of this book are guaranteed to stay active for at least five years from the date of publication.

President

People in Our Government

35

Who Is the President?

The president of the United States is the head of state. This means that he or she is the top leader in the country's government. The president is also in charge of the U.S. armed forces. These groups help keep the country safe.

The United States has had 45 presidents. The first president was George Washington. He led the country from 1789 to 1797. Washington played a key role in building the new country and its government. This is why he is often called the "Father of His Country."

Although George Washington was asked to serve a third term as president, he declined. He did not want the president to rule for a lifetime, like a king would.

The Government

The U.S. government is described in the Constitution. This document was written to establish the new country and its laws. The Constitution explains the three branches of government. Each branch has its own role. Together, they take care of the country and its people.

The legislative branch makes the country's laws. The executive branch carries out the laws. The judicial branch settles any problems with the country's laws.

The three branches of the U.S. government are all based in Washington, D.C. This is the country's capital.

Structure of the U.S. Government

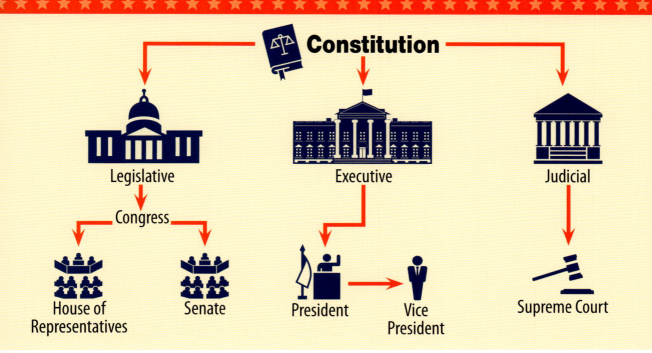

The Role

The president is in charge of the executive branch. Everyone who works in this branch reports to him or her. The president must keep track of what these people are doing. He or she needs to know they are working to help the country.

Another job the president has is to choose people for important jobs. These include **ambassadors** and judges. The president also signs important papers. In 1867, President Andrew Johnson signed the Alaska Treaty. This made Alaska part of the United States.

Presidents meet with ambassadors to learn more about relations with other countries.

Many people thought purchasing Alaska was a poor idea, but they were proven wrong. Today, Alaska is a popular tourist destination.

The United States paid **$7.2 million** for Alaska.

Andrew Johnson was the country's **17th president**.

Theodore Roosevelt is known for helping protect the environment and involving the United States more in world politics.

What It Takes

A person must meet certain rules to become president. He or she must have been born in the United States. Someone who wants to become president must have lived in the country for at least 14 years. No one under the age of 35 can be president.

Theodore Roosevelt was the youngest person to become president. He was 42 years old at the time. Roosevelt took on the role in 1901 when President William McKinley died.

The president must be a U.S. citizen. Anyone born in the United States is a citizen of that country.

Getting the Job

A president is **elected** every four years. However, becoming president does not happen quickly. There are several steps involved.

1 **Candidates** from each **political party** travel the country to gain support. Party members in each state choose the candidate they want to be president.

2 Large meetings are held. Each **political party** chooses one person to run for president.

3 These **nominees** travel across the country. They make speeches and try to get support.

4 People across the country vote for the person they think should be president. Their votes are called the popular vote.

5 Each state has people called electors. The votes of the electors decide which candidate becomes president. The person with the highest popular vote in each state gets that state's electoral votes. The person with the most electoral votes across the country becomes president.

45

The White House

The White House is the official home of the president. This building is found in Washington, D.C. The White House is not just a home. Inside are the offices for the president and his or her staff. There are also rooms for special events.

The State Floor
This is the first floor of the White House. It features the Blue Room. The president uses this room to greet guests. The State Dining Room is also on this floor.

The State Dining Room can seat up to **140 people.**

The White House has **132** rooms, **35** bathrooms, **412** doors, and **28** fireplaces.

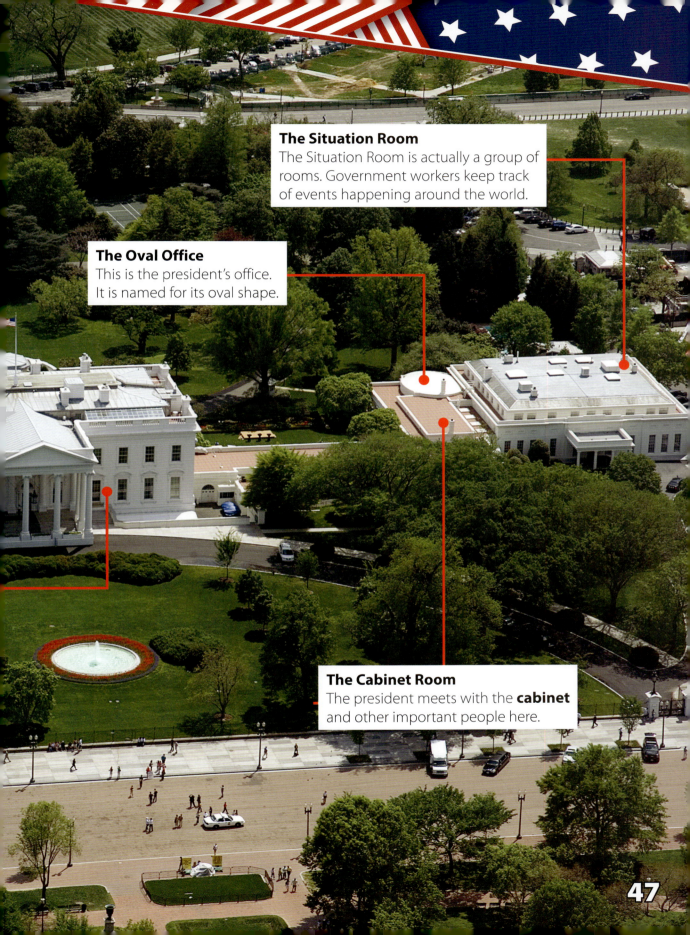

The Situation Room
The Situation Room is actually a group of rooms. Government workers keep track of events happening around the world.

The Oval Office
This is the president's office. It is named for its oval shape.

The Cabinet Room
The president meets with the **cabinet** and other important people here.

47

Leading in Public

Americans look to the president to lead them. The president must keep in touch with them. This is done in a variety of ways.

The president visits states that have been impacted by a natural disaster, such as a hurricane or tornado.

Visits to States

The president travels around the country. He or she speaks with Americans to learn about their problems. The president then returns to Washington to address their concerns.

State of the Union Address

Every year, the president gives a speech about the country. He or she talks about what has been achieved in the last year and what issues need to be addressed in the coming year. This speech is watched on television by tens of millions of people.

The president gives the State of the Union Address from the House Chamber in the U.S. Capitol Building.

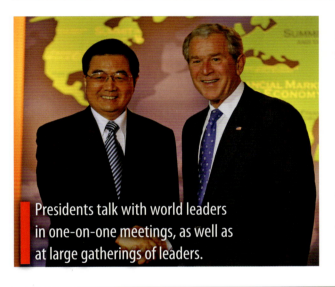

Presidents talk with world leaders in one-on-one meetings, as well as at large gatherings of leaders.

Meets with World Leaders

Helping to solve big problems is part of a president's job. He or she meets with world leaders. They try to resolve issues that affect both the world and the United States.

Celebrates American Victories

The president supports American sports teams. He or she often invites winning teams to the White House. This includes winners of events such as the Super Bowl or the World Series.

The winning team often gives the president a personalized jersey when it visits the White House.

A Day in the Life

The president is a busy person. A president's work never really stops. Each day is filled with questions that need answers.

The president participates in meetings and signs important paperwork at his desk in the Oval Office.

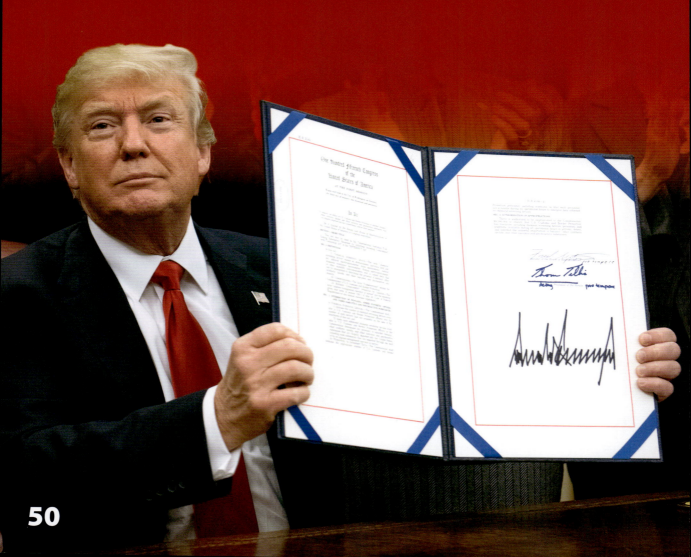

8:00 am	The president and his secretary meet to go over the plans for the day.
9:00 am	The president meets with the head of the National Security Agency. He is given an update on its work.
11:00 am	The governor of Louisiana meets with the president. They discuss the steps being taken to recover from a recent hurricane.
2:00 pm	The president holds a **press conference** to talk about a new **trade** agreement.
4:00 pm	The afternoon includes meetings with the president's staff. There are problems to discuss, such as how to plan a new law.
8:00 pm	The president calls the leader of another country. They discuss how each country can help the other.

Notable Presidents

Presidents are remembered for what they did while in office. Many have taken important actions to help the country grow. Some have also helped the world as a whole.

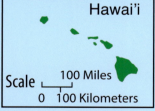

Dwight D. Eisenhower
Years in Office: 1953–1961

Eisenhower is best known for founding **NASA**. He also brought an end to the Korean War. Eisenhower believed in world peace.

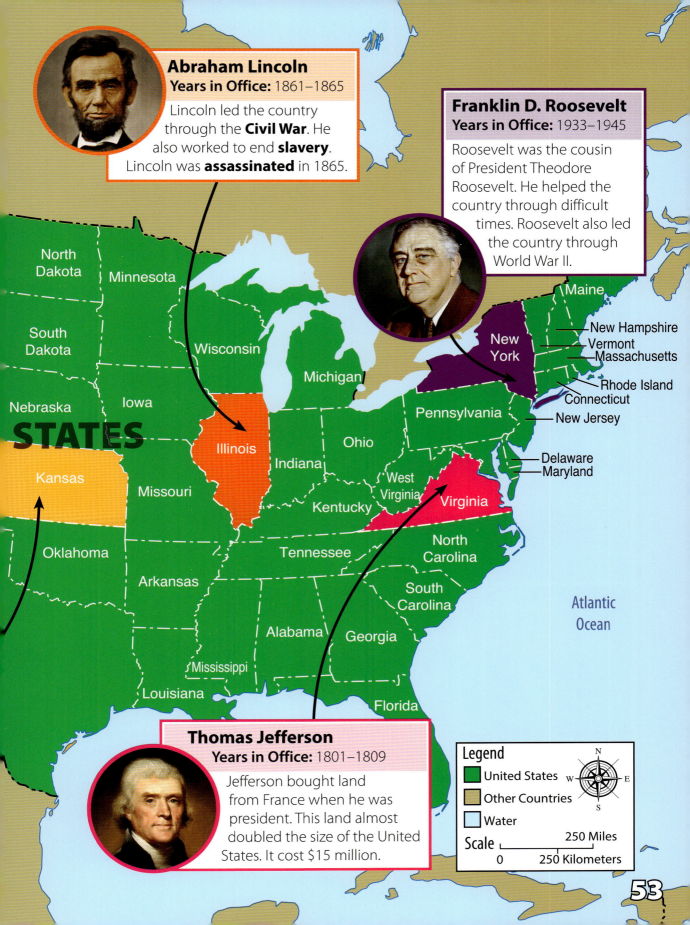

Quiz

1 Who was the first president of the United States?

2 Who is in charge of the executive branch of the U.S. government?

3 How old must someone be to become president?

4 How often is a president elected?

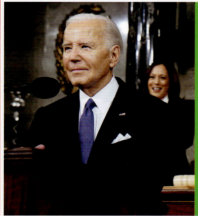

5 What is the State of the Union Address?

6 Which president founded NASA?

ANSWERS
1 George Washington **2** The president **3** At least 35 years old **4** Every four years **5** A speech the president gives about issues facing the country and how to address them **6** Dwight D. Eisenhower

54

Key Words

ambassadors: people who represent their country in another country

assassinated: murdered for political reasons

cabinet: a group of people that gives advice to a leader

candidates: people who seek or are put forward for a job

Civil War: the war between the northern and southern states between 1861 and 1865

elected: voted into a job

NASA: the National Aeronautics and Space Administration, an organization that studies and explores space

nominees: people who are formally entered as a candidate for political office

political party: a group of people who share the same views about the way power should be used in a country

press conference: an event organized to provide information and answer questions from the media

slavery: the practice of owning a person

trade: the business of buying and selling goods

Index (Nonfiction)

Alaska 40, 41
armed forces 36

Constitution 38, 39

Eisenhower, Dwight D. 52, 54
elected 44, 54
executive branch 38, 39, 40, 54

Jefferson, Thomas 53
Johnson, Andrew 40, 41
judicial branch 38, 39

legislative branch 38, 39
Lincoln, Abraham 53

McKinley, William 43

Roosevelt, Franklin D. 53
Roosevelt, Theodore 42, 43, 53

State of the Union Address 49, 54

Washington, D.C. 38, 46, 48
Washington, George 36, 37, 54
White House 46, 49

➕ SUPPLEMENTARY RESOURCES

Click on the plus icon ➕ found in the bottom left corner of each spread to open additional teacher resources.

- Download and print the book's quizzes and activities
- Access curriculum correlations
- Explore additional web applications that enhance the Lightbox experience

LIGHTBOX DIGITAL TITLES
Packed full of integrated media

VIDEOS

INTERACTIVE MAPS

WEBLINKS

SLIDESHOWS

QUIZZES

OPTIMIZED FOR
- ✓ TABLETS
- ✓ SMART BOARDS
- ✓ COMPUTERS
- ✓ AND MUCH MORE!

Published by Lightbox Learning Inc.
276 5th Avenue, Suite 704 #917
New York, NY 10001
Website: www.openlightbox.com

If I Ran for President
First Published by
Albert Whitman & Co.

President
First Published by
LIGHTBOX

If I Ran for President
Written by Catherine Stier, illustrated by Lynne Avril
Text copyright ©2007 by Catherine Stier
Illustrations copyright ©2007 by Lynne Avril
Published by arrangement with Albert Whitman & Company

If I Ran for President first published in the United States of America in 2007 by Albert Whitman & Company, 250 South Northwest Highway, Suite 320, Park Ridge, Illinois 60068 USA
ALL RIGHTS RESERVED

Lightbox Learning acknowledges Getty Images and Shutterstock as the primary image suppliers for the Lightbox *President* title.

Copyright ©2026 Lightbox Learning Inc.
All rights reserved. No part of this publication may be reproduced, stored in a retrieval system, or transmitted in any form or by any means, electronic, mechanical, photocopying, recording, or otherwise, without the prior written permission of the publisher.

Library of Congress Control Number: 2024948064

ISBN 979-8-8745-1974-2 (hardcover)
ISBN 979-8-8745-1973-5 (softcover)
ISBN 979-8-8745-1972-8 (multi-user static eBook)
ISBN 979-8-8745-1970-4 (multi-user interactive eBook)

Printed in Guangzhou, China
1 2 3 4 5 6 7 8 9 0 28 27 26 25 24

112024
102724

Project Coordinator: Priyanka Das
Art Director: Terry Paulhus
Layout: Jean Faye Rodriguez